THIS IS THE RECORD
AND HISTORY OF THE

_____

FAMILY

COMPILED BY:

_____

BEGUN ON:

_____

NELSON REGENCY

ISBN: 0-8407-2323-7

Published in Nashville, Tennessee, by Thomas Nelson, Inc., Publishers.

Printed in the United States of America

299

TABLE OF CONTENTS

HOW TO USE THIS BOOK

Ancestral Charts appear for both the husband and wife at the beginning of this book. Every chart entry has a space for noting the page in this book where a more detailed individual history of that person may be found. Pages are provided for children's histories so that information may be recorded now for future generations.

The individual history pages are designed not only to record facts but also to allow a more complete picture of each person's life. For the longer stories provided by some family members, you may want to use the pages in "Oral History" and "Other Notes." The following page offers tips for getting detailed stories.

The section titled "Important Family Dates (by month)" provides a monthly summary for both important recurrent dates (such as birthdays and anniversaries) and one-time-only events noted with a complete date.

You can probably record a great deal of information about your immediate family right away. Other information may require extended investigative work on your part. To help you uncover "lost" family information, "Resources For Family History" is included at the end of this journal.

You will also notice that a brief history of events and lifestyle changes begins to appear on page 10. These historical notes run from 1989 back to 1900. Recalling a few facts about a period of time may help family members recall their own life details more clearly and generate some interesting stories.

TIPS FOR HELPING
FAMILY MEMBERS REMEMBER

If you have received a blank stare or a shrug of the shoulders when you have asked an elder to tell you about life in "the old days," you may be puzzled about how to get at the colorful details of other's lives. Here are a few tips to help you unlock the stories others have to tell.

- Get the person you are talking with to think about specific incidents, not life in general. For example, ask if he or she can tell you about his or her most memorable Christmas or birthday. What were typical presents and what refreshments were served? Who was the oldest relative at family gatherings? Who was the relative no one liked to talk about?

- Ask to see the person's family photos or scrapbooks. Use pictures or memorabilia to generate stories. Ask when interesting pictures were taken and by whom.

- Ask the person you are interviewing about a typical day at various stages of that person's life. For example, "What was a typical school day like?" or "What did you do on your first day of your first job?"

- Use the Husband's or Wife's History questions to get basic information from the person being interviewed.

- Ask about those relatives or acquaintances who had the most influence in the life of the person you are interviewing.

- Use the historical notes found throughout this journal to stir the memory of your subject.

HUSBAND'S ANCESTRAL CHART

Husband's great grandfather
(see page   )

Husband's grandfather
(see page   )

Husband's great grandmother
(see page   )

Husband's father
(see page 28)

Husband's great grandfather
(see page   )

Husband's grandmother
(see page   )

Husband's great grandmother
(see page   )

Husband's Ancestry
(see page 10)

Husband's great grandfather
(see page   )

Husband's grandfather
(see page   )

Husband's great grandmother
(see page   )

Husband's mother
(see page 30)

Husband's great grandfather
(see page   )

Husband's grandmother
(see page   )

Husband's great grandmother
(see page   )

Husband's great great grandfather (see page   )

Husband's great great grandmother (see page   )

Husband's great great grandfather (see page   )

Husband's great great grandmother (see page   )

Husband's great great grandfather (see page   )

Husband's great great grandmother (see page   )

Husband's great great grandfather (see page   )

Husband's great great grandmother (see page   )

Husband's great great grandfather (see page   )

Husband's great great grandmother (see page   )

Husband's great great grandfather (see page   )

Husband's great great grandmother (see page   )

Husband's great great grandfather (see page   )

Husband's great great grandmother (see page   )

Husband's great great grandfather (see page   )

Husband's great great grandmother (see page   )

| Husband's great great great grandfather (see page   ) |
| Husband's great great great grandmother (see page   ) |
| Husband's great great great grandfather (see page   ) |
| Husband's great great great grandmother (see page   ) |
| Husband's great great great grandfather (see page   ) |
| Husband's great great great grandmother (see page   ) |
| Husband's great great great grandfather (see page   ) |
| Husband's great great great grandmother (see page   ) |
| Husband's great great great grandfather (see page   ) |
| Husband's great great great grandmother (see page   ) |
| Husband's great great great grandfather (see page   ) |
| Husband's great great great grandmother (see page   ) |
| Husband's great great great grandfather (see page   ) |
| Husband's great great great grandmother (see page   ) |
| Husband's great great great grandfather (see page   ) |
| Husband's great great great grandmother (see page   ) |
| Husband's great great great grandfather (see page   ) |
| Husband's great great great grandmother (see page   ) |
| Husband's great great great grandfather (see page   ) |
| Husband's great great great grandmother (see page   ) |
| Husband's great great great grandfather (see page   ) |
| Husband's great great great grandmother (see page   ) |
| Husband's great great great grandfather (see page   ) |
| Husband's great great great grandmother (see page   ) |
| Husband's great great great grandfather (see page   ) |
| Husband's great great great grandmother (see page   ) |
| Husband's great great great grandfather (see page   ) |
| Husband's great great great grandmother (see page   ) |
| Husband's great great great grandfather (see page   ) |
| Husband's great great great grandmother (see page   ) |
| Husband's great great great grandfather (see page   ) |
| Husband's great great great grandmother (see page   ) |

WIFE'S ANCESTRAL CHART

Wife's great grandfather
(see page   )

Wife's grandfather
(see page   )

Wife's great grandmother
(see page   )

Wife's father
(see page 32)

Wife's great grandfather
(see page   )

Wife's grandmother
(see page   )

Wife's great grandmother
(see page   )

Wife's Ancestry
(see page 12)

Wife's great grandfather
(see page   )

Wife's grandfather
(see page   )

Wife's great grandmother
(see page   )

Wife's mother
(see page 34)

Wife's great grandfather
(see page   )

Wife's grandmother
(see page   )

Wife's great grandmother
(see page   )

8

Wife's great great grandfather (see page   )

Wife's great great great grandfather (see page   )

Wife's great great great grandmother (see page   )

Wife's great great grandmother (see page   )

Wife's great great great grandfather (see page   )

Wife's great great great grandmother (see page   )

Wife's great great grandfather (see page   )

Wife's great great great grandfather (see page   )

Wife's great great great grandmother (see page   )

Wife's great great grandmother (see page   )

Wife's great great great grandfather (see page   )

Wife's great great great grandmother (see page   )

Wife's great great grandfather (see page   )

Wife's great great great grandfather (see page   )

Wife's great great great grandmother (see page   )

Wife's great great grandmother (see page   )

Wife's great great great grandfather (see page   )

Wife's great great great grandmother (see page   )

Wife's great great grandfather (see page   )

Wife's great great great grandfather (see page   )

Wife's great great great grandmother (see page   )

Wife's great great grandmother (see page   )

Wife's great great great grandfather (see page   )

Wife's great great great grandmother (see page   )

Wife's great great grandfather (see page   )

Wife's great great great grandfather (see page   )

Wife's great great great grandmother (see page   )

Wife's great great grandmother (see page   )

Wife's great great great grandfather (see page   )

Wife's great great great grandmother (see page   )

Wife's great great grandfather (see page   )

Wife's great great great grandfather (see page   )

Wife's great great great grandmother (see page   )

Wife's great great grandmother (see page   )

Wife's great great great grandfather (see page   )

Wife's great great great grandmother (see page   )

Wife's great great grandfather (see page   )

Wife's great great great grandfather (see page   )

Wife's great great great grandmother (see page   )

Wife's great great grandmother (see page   )

Wife's great great great grandfather (see page   )

Wife's great great great grandmother (see page   )

HUSBAND'S HISTORY

Husband's
photo goes
here

Full name _____
Date of birth _____
Place of birth _____
Size at birth _____
Hair color _____
Eye color _____
Mother's full name _____
Father's full name _____
Siblings (name & date of birth) _____
_____
_____

Marriage date and place _____
    Groomsmen _____
    Special notes _____
_____

Schools, degrees, courses of study _____
_____
_____
_____

Occupation(s) and employment (including military service) _____
_____
_____
_____

Places lived (most current to first home) _____
_____

Lifestyle in the 1980s
Fitness becomes a foremost goal of
"yuppies"; communications technology
gives us cellular phones and FAX machines.
MTV moves into U.S. households.

Religious affiliations _____

Honors & achievements _____

Organizations joined _____

Favorite sports/hobbies _____

Best friends (including age when met) _____

Pets owned _____

Vehicles owned _____

Other interesting facts and stories _____

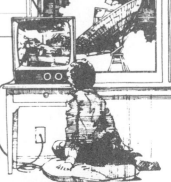

1989
After a 12-year journey in space, the
Voyager 2 sends remarkable pictures of the
planet Neptune back to U.S. scientists.

WIFE'S HISTORY

Wife's
photo goes
here

Full name _____

Date of birth _____

Place of birth _____

Size at birth _____

Hair color _____

Eye color _____

Mother's full name _____

Father's full name _____

Siblings (name & date of birth) _____

_____

_____

Marriage date and place _____

Bridesmaids _____

Special notes _____

Schools, degrees, courses of study _____

_____

_____

Occupation(s) and employment (including military service) _____

_____

_____

Places lived (most current to first home) _____

_____

_____

November 9, 1989
The Berlin Wall is opened and thousands of
East Germans pour into the West.

Religious affiliations _____

_____

Honors & achievements _____

_____

_____

Organizations joined _____

_____

_____

Favorite sports/hobbies _____

_____

_____

Best friends (including age when met) _____

_____

_____

_____

Pets owned _____

_____

Vehicles owned _____

_____

Other interesting facts and stories _____

_____

_____

July, 1988 At the Democratic Convention, Jesse Jackson is the first black man to make a serious bid for the U.S. Presidency.

CHILD'S HISTORY

Child's
photo goes
here

Full name _____

Date & time of birth _____

Place of birth _____

Size at birth _____

Hair color _____

Eye color _____

Social security number _____

Named after _____

Siblings (name & date of birth) _____

_____

_____

Schools, degrees, courses of study _____

_____

_____

Marriage date and place _____

    Special notes _____

_____

_____

Occupation(s) and employment (including military service) _____

_____

_____

_____

Places lived (most current to first home) _____

_____

_____

_____

_____

December 23, 1986
Voyager, a superlight plane, circles the
globe nonstop without refueling.

Religious affiliations _____
_____

Honors & achievements _____
_____
_____

Organizations joined _____
_____
_____

Favorite sports/hobbies _____
_____
_____

Best friends (including age when met) _____
_____
_____
_____

Pets owned _____
_____

Vehicles owned _____
_____

Other interesting facts and stories _____
_____
_____
_____
_____

July 4, 1986
The 100th birthday of the Statue of Liberty.

CHILD'S HISTORY

Child's
photo goes
here

Full name _____

Date & time of birth _____

Place of birth _____

Size at birth _____

Hair color _____

Eye color _____

Social security number _____

Named after _____

Siblings (name & date of birth) _____

_____

_____

_____

Schools, degrees, courses of study _____

_____

_____

Marriage date and place _____

Special notes _____

_____

Occupation(s) and employment (including military service) _____

_____

_____

_____

Places lived (most current to first home) _____

_____

_____

_____

July 13, 1985
"Live Aid" brings out international rock stars
to raise money for famine relief.

Religious affiliations _____

_____

Honors & achievements _____

_____

_____

Organizations joined _____

_____

_____

Favorite sports/hobbies _____

_____

_____

Best friends (including age when met) _____

_____

_____

_____

Pets owned _____

_____

Vehicles owned _____

_____

Other interesting facts and stories _____

_____

_____

_____

July 12, 1984
Geraldine Ferraro becomes the first woman
Vice Presidential candidate on a major
party ticket.

CHILD'S HISTORY

Child's
photo goes
here

Full name _____

Date & time of birth _____

Place of birth _____

Size at birth _____

Hair color _____

Eye color _____

Social security number _____

Named after _____

Siblings (name & date of birth) _____

_____

_____

Schools, degrees, courses of study _____

_____

_____

Marriage date and place _____

Special notes _____

_____

Occupation(s) and employment (including military service) _____

_____

_____

_____

Places lived (most current to first home) _____

_____

_____

June 18, 1983
Sally Ride becomes the first U.S. woman
in space.

Religious affiliations _____

_____

Honors & achievements _____

_____

_____

Organizations joined _____

_____

_____

Favorite sports/hobbies _____

_____

_____

Best friends (including age when met) _____

_____

_____

_____

Pets owned _____

_____

Vehicles owned _____

_____

Other interesting facts and stories _____

_____

_____

December 22, 1982
The first permanent artificial heart surgery is performed.

19

CHILD'S HISTORY ✿◆✿◆✿◆

Child's
photo goes
here

Full name _____

Date & time of birth _____

Place of birth _____

Size at birth _____

Hair color _____

Eye color _____

Social security number _____

Named after _____

Siblings (name & date of birth) _____

_____

_____

Schools, degrees, courses of study _____

_____

_____

Marriage date and place _____

Special notes _____

_____

Occupation(s) and employment (including military service) _____

_____

_____

_____

Places lived (most current to first home) _____

_____

_____

_____

January 31, 1980
Iran releases American hostages after 444
days of captivity.

Religious affiliations _____

_____

_____

Honors & achievements _____

_____

_____

_____

Organizations joined _____

_____

_____

_____

Favorite sports/hobbies _____

_____

_____

_____

Best friends (including age when met) _____

_____

_____

_____

_____

_____

Pets owned _____

_____

_____

Vehicles owned _____

_____

_____

Other interesting facts and stories _____

_____

_____

_____

_____

The 1980s

Drugs, the homeless and AIDS are major concerns. Environmental issues are taken up by the general public. Recycling, ozone depletion and the greenhouse effect become household words.

CHILD'S HISTORY 🐎 🐎 🐎 🐎

Child's
photo goes
here

Full name _____

Date & time of birth _____

Place of birth _____

Size at birth _____

Hair color _____

Eye color _____

Social security number _____

Named after _____

Siblings (name & date of birth) _____

_____

_____

Schools, degrees, courses of study _____

_____

_____

Marriage date and place _____

Special notes _____

_____

Occupation(s) and employment (including military service) _____

_____

_____

_____

Places lived (most current to first home) _____

_____

_____

_____

March 31, 1979
Three Mile Island (Pennsylvania) is the site of the
most serious accident in the history of the U.S.
nuclear reactor program.

Religious affiliations _____

_____

Honors & achievements _____

_____

_____

Organizations joined _____

_____

_____

Favorite sports/hobbies _____

_____

_____

Best friends (including age when met) _____

_____

_____

_____

Pets owned _____

_____

Vehicles owned _____

_____

Other interesting facts and stories _____

_____

_____

July 9, 1978
More than 100,000 march in Washington, D.C. for an
extension to ratify the Equal Rights Amendment.

WEDDINGS

_____ and _____
husband   wife

Date _____ Place _____ Time _____

Ceremony conducted by _____

Attendants _____

_____

Special notes _____

_____

_____

_____ and _____
husband   wife

Date _____ Place _____ Time _____

Ceremony conducted by _____

Attendants _____

_____

Special notes _____

_____

_____

_____ and _____
husband   wife

Date _____ Place _____ Time _____

Ceremony conducted by _____

Attendants _____

_____

Special notes _____

_____

May 22, 1977
Janet Guthrie becomes the first woman driver to qualify for the Indy 500.

_____ and _____
            husband   wife
Date _____ Place _____ Time _____

Ceremony conducted by _____

Attendants _____

_____

Special notes _____

_____

_____

_____ and _____
            husband   wife
Date _____ Place _____ Time _____

Ceremony conducted by _____

Attendants _____

_____

Special notes _____

_____

_____

_____ and _____
            husband   wife
Date _____ Place _____ Time _____

Ceremony conducted by _____

Attendants _____

_____

Special notes _____

_____

1977
Use of CB radios in passenger vehicles hits its peak.

BIRTHS

Name _____ Date and Time _____

Mother _____ Father _____

Place _____

Weight _____ Height _____ Notes _____

Name _____ Date and Time _____

Mother _____ Father _____

Place _____

Weight _____ Height _____ Notes _____

Name _____ Date and Time _____

Mother _____ Father _____

Place _____

Weight _____ Height _____ Notes _____

Name _____ Date and Time _____

Mother _____ Father _____

Place _____

Weight _____ Height _____ Notes _____

Name _____ Date and Time _____

Mother _____ Father _____

Place _____

Weight _____ Height _____ Notes _____

November 2, 1976
Jimmy Carter is elected President.

Name _____ Date and Time_____

Mother _____ Father _____

Place _____

Weight_____ Height_____ Notes_____

Name _____ Date and Time_____

Mother _____ Father _____

Place _____

Weight_____ Height_____ Notes_____

Name _____ Date and Time_____

Mother _____ Father _____

Place _____

Weight_____ Height_____ Notes_____

Name _____ Date and Time_____

Mother _____ Father _____

Place _____

Weight_____ Height_____ Notes_____

Name _____ Date and Time_____

Mother _____ Father _____

Place _____

Weight_____ Height_____ Notes_____

July 4, 1976
The nation celebrates its 200th birthday with tall
ships, parades and fireworks.

HUSBAND'S FATHER'S HISTORY

Husband's
Father's photo goes
here

Full name _____

Date of birth _____

Place of birth _____

Size at birth _____

Hair color _____

Eye color _____

Mother's full name _____

Father's full name _____

Siblings (name & date of birth) _____

_____

_____

Marriage (date, place and special notes) _____

Children (name[s] and birthdate[s]) _____

Schools, degrees, courses of study _____

Occupation[s] and employment (including military service) _____

Places lived (most current to first home) _____

July 17, 1975
Soviet and U.S. spacecrafts link in space.

Religious affiliations

Honors & achievements

Organizations joined

Favorite sports/hobbies

Best friends (including age when met)

Pets owned

Vehicles owned

Other interesting facts and stories

August 9, 1974
Richard M. Nixon becomes the first U.S. President to resign. Vice President Gerald Ford becomes President.

HUSBAND'S MOTHER'S HISTORY

Husband's
Mother's photo goes
here

Full name _____

Date of birth _____

Place of birth _____

Size at birth _____

Hair color _____

Eye color _____

Mother's full name _____

Father's full name _____

Siblings (name & date of birth) _____

_____

_____

Marriage (date, place and special notes) _____

_____

Children (name[s] and birthdate[s]) _____

_____

Schools, degrees, courses of study _____

_____

Occupation[s] and employment (including military service) _____

_____

_____

Places lived (most current to first home) _____

_____

_____

_____

November 7, 1972
In a record-setting victory, President Nixon is
re-elected carrying 49 states.

Religious affiliations

Honors & achievements

Organizations joined

Favorite sports/hobbies

Best friends (including age when met)

Pets owned

Vehicles owned

Other interesting facts and stories

August 12, 1972
U.S. ground troops pull out of Vietnam.

WIFE'S FATHER'S HISTORY

Wife's
Father's photo goes
here

Full name _____

Date of birth _____

Place of birth _____

Size at birth _____

Hair color _____

Eye color _____

Mother's full name _____

Father's full name _____

Siblings (name & date of birth) _____

_____

_____

Marriage (date, place and special notes) _____

_____

Children (name[s] and birthdate[s]) _____

_____

Schools, degrees, courses of study _____

_____

Occupation[s] and employment (including military service) _____

_____

_____

Places lived (most current to first home) _____

_____

June 17, 1972
"Watergate" begins as burglars are arrested in
Democratic National Committee headquarters in the
Watergate building.

Religious affiliations

Honors & achievements

Organizations joined

Favorite sports/hobbies

Best friends (including age when met)

Pets owned

Vehicles owned

Other interesting facts and stories

August 26, 1970
Women's Strike for Equality Day marked the 50th anniversary of the women's suffrage amendment.

33

WIFE'S MOTHER'S HISTORY

Wife's
Mother's photo goes
here

Full name _____

Date of birth _____

Place of birth _____

Size at birth _____

Hair color _____

Eye color _____

Mother's full name _____

Father's full name _____

Siblings (name & date of birth) _____

_____

_____

Marriage (date, place and special notes) _____

_____

Children (name[s] and birthdate[s]) _____

_____

Schools, degrees, courses of study _____

_____

Occupation[s] and employment (including military service) _____

_____

_____

_____

Places lived (most current to first home) _____

_____

_____

_____

1969
The Woodstock Music and Art Fair draws an amazing
400,000 young people and becomes a symbol of
the "Woodstock Generation."

Religious affiliations

Honors & achievements

Organizations joined

Favorite sports/hobbies

Best friends (including age when met)

Pets owned

Vehicles owned

Other interesting facts and stories

July 20, 1969
Astronaut Neil Armstrong becomes the first man to
set foot on the moon.

HUSBAND'S GRANDPARENT'S HISTORY

Husband's
Grandparent's photo
goes here

Full name _____

Date of birth _____

Place of birth _____

Size at birth _____

Hair color _____

Eye color _____

Mother's full name _____

Father's full name _____

Siblings (name & date of birth) _____

_____

_____

Marriage (date, place and special notes) _____

_____

Children (name[s] and birthdate[s]) _____

_____

Schools, degrees, courses of study _____

_____

Occupation[s] and employment (including military service) _____

_____

_____

Places lived (most current to first home) _____

_____

_____

June 5, 1968
Senator Robert F. Kennedy is assassinated.

Religious affiliations _____

Honors & achievements _____

Organizations joined _____

Favorite sports/hobbies _____

Best friends (including age when met) _____

Pets owned _____

Vehicles owned _____

Other interesting facts and stories _____

November 5, 1968
Richard M. Nixon is elected President.

HUSBAND'S GRANDPARENT'S HISTORY

Husband's
Grandparent's photo
goes here

Full name _____

Date of birth _____

Place of birth _____

Size at birth _____

Hair color _____

Eye color _____

Mother's full name _____

Father's full name _____

Siblings (name & date of birth) _____

_____

_____

Marriage (date, place and special notes) _____

_____

Children (name[s] and birthdate[s]) _____

_____

Schools, degrees, courses of study _____

_____

Occupation[s] and employment (including military service) _____

_____

_____

Places lived (most current to first home) _____

_____

_____

April 4, 1968
Dr. Martin Luther King is assassinated.

38

Religious affiliations _____

_____

Honors & achievements _____

_____

_____

Organizations joined _____

_____

_____

Favorite sports/hobbies _____

_____

_____

Best friends (including age when met) _____

_____

_____

_____

Pets owned _____

_____

Vehicles owned _____

_____

Other interesting facts and stories _____

_____

_____

_____

_____

y 2, 1964
U.S. Civil Rights Act prohibiting racial
crimination is signed into law.

39

HUSBAND'S GRANDPARENT'S HISTORY

Husband's
Grandparent's photo
goes here

Full name _____

Date of birth _____

Place of birth _____

Size at birth _____

Hair color _____

Eye color _____

Mother's full name _____

Father's full name _____

Siblings (name & date of birth) _____

_____

_____

Marriage (date, place and special notes) _____

_____

Children (name[s] and birthdate[s]) _____

_____

Schools, degrees, courses of study _____

_____

Occupation[s] and employment (including military service) _____

_____

_____

_____

Places lived (most current to first home) _____

_____

_____

1964
England's phenomenal rock group, The Beatles,
invade America.

40

Religious affiliations

Honors & achievements

Organizations joined

Favorite sports/hobbies

Best friends (including age when met)

Pets owned

Vehicles owned

Other interesting facts and stories

November 22, 1963
President Kennedy is assassinated in Dallas and Vice
President Lyndon B. Johnson assumes the Presidency.

HUSBAND'S GRANDPARENT'S HISTORY

Husband's
Grandparent's photo
goes here

Full name _____
Date of birth _____
Place of birth _____
Size at birth _____
Hair color _____
Eye color _____
Mother's full name _____
Father's full name _____
Siblings (name & date of birth) _____
_____
_____
_____

Marriage (date, place and special notes) _____
_____

Children (name[s] and birthdate[s]) _____
_____

Schools, degrees, courses of study _____
_____

Occupation[s] and employment (including military service) _____
_____
_____

Places lived (most current to first home) _____
_____

February 20, 1962
John Glenn becomes the first U.S. astronaut to orbit the Earth.

42

Religious affiliations _____

_____

Honors & achievements _____

_____

_____

Organizations joined _____

_____

_____

Favorite sports/hobbies _____

_____

_____

Best friends (including age when met) _____

_____

_____

_____

Pets owned _____

_____

Vehicles owned _____

_____

Other interesting facts and stories _____

_____

_____

_____

_____

August 17, 1961
The Berlin Wall goes up in East Germany to prevent
refugees from crossing to the west.

WIFE'S GRANDPARENT'S HISTORY

Wife's
Grandparent's photo
goes here

Full name _____

Date of birth _____

Place of birth _____

Size at birth _____

Hair color _____

Eye color _____

Mother's full name _____

Father's full name _____

Siblings (name & date of birth) _____

_____

_____

Marriage (date, place and special notes) _____

_____

Children (name[s] and birthdate[s]) _____

_____

Schools, degrees, courses of study _____

_____

Occupation[s] and employment (including military service) _____

_____

_____

Places lived (most current to first home) _____

_____

_____

April 12, 1961
The Soviet Union successfully puts a manned
spacecraft into Earth's orbit.

Religious affiliations

Honors & achievements

Organizations joined

Favorite sports/hobbies

Best friends (including age when met)

Pets owned

Vehicles owned

Other interesting facts and stories

November 8, 1960
John F. Kennedy becomes President.

WIFE'S GRANDPARENT'S HISTORY

Wife's
Grandparent's photo
goes here

Full name _____

Date of birth _____

Place of birth _____

Size at birth _____

Hair color _____

Eye color _____

Mother's full name _____

Father's full name _____

Siblings (name & date of birth) _____

_____

_____

Marriage (date, place and special notes) _____

_____

Children (name[s] and birthdate[s]) _____

_____

Schools, degrees, courses of study _____

_____

Occupation[s] and employment (including military service) _____

_____

_____

Places lived (most current to first home) _____

_____

_____

_____

1958
Hula-hoops become a hot fad, and "cramming" or "stuffing" to get the most people into a small space (such as a telephone booth) is the rage on college campuses.

Religious affiliations _____

_____

Honors & achievements _____

_____

_____

Organizations joined _____

_____

_____

Favorite sports/hobbies _____

_____

_____

Best friends (including age when met) _____

_____

_____

_____

Pets owned _____

_____

Vehicles owned _____

_____

Other interesting facts and stories _____

_____

_____

_____

August 21, 1958
Hawaii becomes the 50th state.

47

WIFE'S GRANDPARENT'S HISTORY

Wife's
Grandparent's photo
goes here

Full name _____
Date of birth _____
Place of birth _____
Size at birth _____
Hair color _____
Eye color _____
Mother's full name _____
Father's full name _____
Siblings (name & date of birth) ____
_____
_____

Marriage (date, place and special notes) _____
_____

Children (name[s] and birthdate[s]) _____
_____

Schools, degrees, courses of study _____
_____

Occupation[s] and employment (including military service) _____
_____
_____

Places lived (most current to first home) _____
_____
_____
_____

February 1, 1958
The U.S. puts its first satellite, Explorer I,
into the Earth's orbit.

48

Religious affiliations _____

_____

Honors & achievements _____

_____

_____

Organizations joined _____

_____

_____

Favorite sports/hobbies _____

_____

_____

Best friends (including age when met) _____

_____

_____

_____

Pets owned _____

_____

Vehicles owned _____

_____

Other interesting facts and stories _____

_____

_____

_____

_____

August 26, 1957
Ford introduces the Edsel.

WIFE'S GRANDPARENT'S HISTORY

Wife's
Grandparent's photo
goes here

Full name _____
Date of birth _____
Place of birth _____
Size at birth _____
Hair color _____
Eye color _____
Mother's full name _____
Father's full name _____
Siblings (name & date of birth) _____
_____
_____

Marriage (date, place and special notes) _____
_____

Children (name[s] and birthdate[s]) _____
_____

Schools, degrees, courses of study _____
_____

Occupation[s] and employment (including military service) _____
_____
_____

Places lived (most current to first home) _____
_____
_____
_____

1955
Rebel Without a Cause establishes James Dean
as the symbol of rebellion among teenagers.

Religious affiliations _____

_____

_____

Honors & achievements _____

_____

_____

_____

Organizations joined _____

_____

_____

_____

Favorite sports/hobbies _____

_____

_____

_____

Best friends (including age when met) _____

_____

_____

_____

_____

_____

Pets owned _____

_____

Vehicles owned _____

_____

_____

Other interesting facts and stories _____

_____

_____

_____

1955
Dr. Martin Luther King gains public attention as a
civil rights activist.

51

Great
Grandparent's
photo goes
here

Full name _____
Date of birth _____
Place of birth _____
Size at birth _____
Hair color _____
Eye color _____
Mother's full name _____
Father's full name _____
Siblings (name & date of birth) _____
_____
_____

Marriage (date, place and special notes) _____

Children (name[s] and birthdate[s]) _____

Schools, degrees, courses of study _____

Occupation[s] and employment (including military service) _____
_____

Places lived (most current to first home) _____
_____

Religious affiliations _____

Honors & achievements _____

Other interesting facts and stories _____
_____

1954 Segregation in public schools is ruled unconstitutional by the U.S. Supreme Court.

52

GREAT GRANDPARENT'S HISTORY

Great
Grandparent's
photo goes
here

Full name _____

Date of birth _____

Place of birth _____

Size at birth _____

Hair color _____

Eye color _____

Mother's full name _____

Father's full name _____

Siblings (name & date of birth) _____

_____

_____

Marriage (date, place and special notes) _____

_____

Children (name[s] and birthdate[s]) _____

_____

Schools, degrees, courses of study _____

_____

Occupation[s] and employment (including military service) _____

_____

_____

Places lived (most current to first home) _____

_____

_____

Religious affiliations _____

Honors & achievements _____

_____

Other interesting facts and stories _____

_____

1954
The Salk polio vaccine goes into
widespread use.

53

_____ GREAT GRANDPARENT'S HISTORY

Great
Grandparent's
photo goes
here

Full name _____

Date of birth _____

Place of birth _____

Size at birth _____

Hair color _____

Eye color _____

Mother's full name _____

Father's full name _____

Siblings (name & date of birth) _____

_____

Marriage (date, place and special notes) _____

Children (name[s] and birthdate[s]) _____

Schools, degrees, courses of study _____

Occupation[s] and employment (including military service) _____

_____

Places lived (most current to first home) _____

_____

Religious affiliations _____

Honors & achievements _____

Other interesting facts and stories _____

_____

_____

1952
3-D movies are introduced.

GREAT GRANDPARENT'S HISTORY

Great
Grandparent's
photo goes
here

Full name _____

Date of birth _____

Place of birth _____

Size at birth _____

Hair color _____

Eye color _____

Mother's full name _____

Father's full name _____

Siblings (name & date of birth) _____

_____

_____

Marriage (date, place and special notes) _____

Children (name[s] and birthdate[s]) _____

Schools, degrees, courses of study _____

Occupation[s] and employment (including military service) _____

_____

Places lived (most current to first home) _____

_____

Religious affiliations _____

Honors & achievements _____

Other interesting facts and stories _____

_____

November 4, 1952
Dwight D. Eisenhower becomes President.

55

Great Grandparent's photo goes here

Full name _____

Date of birth _____

Place of birth _____

Size at birth _____

Hair color _____

Eye color _____

Mother's full name _____

Father's full name _____

Siblings (name & date of birth) _____

_____

_____

Marriage (date, place and special notes) _____

Children (name[s] and birthdate[s]) _____

Schools, degrees, courses of study _____

Occupation[s] and employment (including military service) _____

_____

Places lived (most current to first home) _____

_____

Religious affiliations _____

Honors & achievements _____

Other interesting facts and stories _____

1950
The first computer developed for commercial use is called the Univac I.

GREAT GRANDPARENT'S HISTORY

Great
Grandparent's
photo goes
here

Full name _____

Date of birth _____

Place of birth _____

Size at birth _____

Hair color _____

Eye color _____

Mother's full name _____

Father's full name _____

Siblings (name & date of birth) _____

_____

_____

Marriage (date, place and special notes) _____

Children (name[s] and birthdate[s]) _____

Schools, degrees, courses of study _____

Occupation[s] and employment (including military service) _____

_____

Places lived (most current to first home) _____

_____

Religious affiliations _____

Honors & achievements _____

Other interesting facts and stories _____

The 1950s
The development of the suburban lifestyle,
television sets in most households, the station
wagon, fallout shelters, and an increased church
membership.

_____ GREAT GRANDPARENT'S HISTORY

Great
Grandparent's
photo goes
here

Full name _____

Date of birth _____

Place of birth _____

Size at birth _____

Hair color _____

Eye color _____

Mother's full name _____

Father's full name _____

Siblings (name & date of birth) _____

_____

_____

Marriage (date, place and special notes) _____

Children (name[s] and birthdate[s]) _____

Schools, degrees, courses of study _____

Occupation[s] and employment (including military service) _____

_____

Places lived (most current to first home) _____

_____

Religious affiliations _____

Honors & achievements _____

Other interesting facts and stories _____

_____

_____

1948

LPs (long playing records) sound off in the U.S.

_____ GREAT GRANDPARENT'S HISTORY

Great
Grandparent's
photo goes
here

Full name _____

Date of birth _____

Place of birth _____

Size at birth _____

Hair color _____

Eye color _____

Mother's full name _____

Father's full name _____

Siblings (name & date of birth) _____

_____

_____

Marriage (date, place and special notes) _____

Children (name[s] and birthdate[s]) _____

Schools, degrees, courses of study _____

Occupation[s] and employment (including military service) _____

_____

Places lived (most current to first home) _____

_____

Religious affiliations _____

Honors & achievements _____

Other interesting facts and stories _____

_____

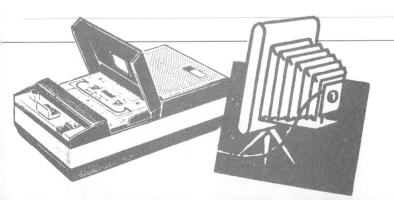

1947 Tape recorders become available for home use, and the Polaroid Land Camera is invented.

GREAT GRANDPARENT'S HISTORY

Full name _____

Date of birth _____

Place of birth _____

Size at birth _____

Hair color _____

Great
Grandparent's
photo goes
here

Eye color _____

Mother's full name _____

Father's full name _____

Siblings (name & date of birth) _____

_____

_____

Marriage (date, place and special notes) _____

_____

Children (name[s] and birthdate[s]) _____

_____

Schools, degrees, courses of study _____

_____

Occupation[s] and employment (including military service) _____

_____

_____

Places lived (most current to first home) _____

_____

_____

Religious affiliations _____

_____

Honors & achievements _____

_____

Other interesting facts and stories _____

_____

_____

_____

August 14, 1945
Japan surrenders. The surrender is formally signed
on September 2.

60

GREAT GRANDPARENT'S HISTORY

Great
Grandparent's
photo goes
here

Full name _____

Date of birth _____

Place of birth _____

Size at birth _____

Hair color _____

Eye color _____

Mother's full name _____

Father's full name _____

Siblings (name & date of birth) _____

_____

_____

Marriage (date, place and special notes) _____

_____

Children (name[s] and birthdate[s]) _____

_____

Schools, degrees, courses of study _____

_____

Occupation[s] and employment (including military service) _____

_____

_____

Places lived (most current to first home) _____

_____

_____

Religious affiliations _____

_____

Honors & achievements _____

_____

Other interesting facts and stories _____

August 6, 1945
The U.S. drops the first atomic bomb on Hiroshima.

_____ GREAT GRANDPARENT'S HISTORY

Great
Grandparent's
photo goes
here

Full name _____

Date of birth _____

Place of birth _____

Size at birth _____

Hair color _____

Eye color _____

Mother's full name _____

Father's full name _____

Siblings (name & date of birth) _____

_____

Marriage (date, place and special notes) _____

Children (name[s] and birthdate[s]) _____

Schools, degrees, courses of study _____

Occupation[s] and employment (including military service) _____

_____

Places lived (most current to first home) _____

_____

Religious affiliations _____

Honors & achievements _____

Other interesting facts and stories _____

_____

April 30, 1945
Hitler commits suicide. Berlin is surrendered two days later.

GREAT GRANDPARENT'S HISTORY

Great
Grandparent's
photo goes
here

Full name
Date of birth
Place of birth
Size at birth
Hair color
Eye color
Mother's full name
Father's full name
Siblings (name & date of birth)

Marriage (date, place and special notes)

Children (name[s] and birthdate[s])

Schools, degrees, courses of study

Occupation[s] and employment (including military service)

Places lived (most current to first home)

Religious affiliations

Honors & achievements

Other interesting facts and stories

April 12, 1945
Vice President Harry S. Truman becomes President
when Roosevelt dies of a cerebral hemorrhage.

Great
Grandparent's
photo goes
here

Full name _____

Date of birth _____

Place of birth _____

Size at birth _____

Hair color _____

Eye color _____

Mother's full name _____

Father's full name _____

Siblings (name & date of birth) _____

_____

_____

Marriage (date, place and special notes) _____

_____

Children (name[s] and birthdate[s]) _____

_____

Schools, degrees, courses of study _____

_____

Occupation[s] and employment (including military service) _____

_____

_____

Places lived (most current to first home) _____

_____

_____

Religious affiliations _____

_____

Honors & achievements _____

_____

Other interesting facts and stories _____

_____

November 7, 1944
Franklin Roosevelt is elected to his fourth term
as President.

GREAT GRANDPARENT'S HISTORY

Great
Grandparent's
photo goes
here

Full name _____
Date of birth _____
Place of birth _____
Size at birth _____
Hair color _____
Eye color _____
Mother's full name _____
Father's full name _____
Siblings (name & date of birth) _____
_____
_____

Marriage (date, place and special notes) _____

Children (name[s] and birthdate[s]) _____

Schools, degrees, courses of study _____

Occupation[s] and employment (including military service) _____
_____

Places lived (most current to first home) _____
_____

Religious affiliations _____

Honors & achievements _____

Other interesting facts and stories _____
_____

June 6, 1944
D-Day, the beginning of the final assault against
Hitler in Europe.

GREAT GRANDPARENT'S HISTORY

Great
Grandparent's
photo goes
here

Full name _____

Date of birth _____

Place of birth _____

Size at birth _____

Hair color _____

Eye color _____

Mother's full name _____

Father's full name _____

Siblings (name & date of birth) _____

_____

_____

Marriage (date, place and special notes) _____

Children (name[s] and birthdate[s]) _____

Schools, degrees, courses of study _____

Occupation[s] and employment (including military service) _____

_____

Places lived (most current to first home) _____

_____

Religious affiliations _____

Honors & achievements _____

Other interesting facts and stories _____

1943
The Rodgers and Hammerstein musical
"Oklahoma" opens on Broadway.

GREAT GRANDPARENT'S HISTORY

Great
Grandparent's
photo goes
here

Full name _____
Date of birth _____
Place of birth _____
Size at birth _____
Hair color _____
Eye color _____
Mother's full name _____
Father's full name _____
Siblings (name & date of birth) _____
_____
_____

Marriage (date, place and special notes) _____

Children (name[s] and birthdate[s]) _____

Schools, degrees, courses of study _____

Occupation[s] and employment (including military service) _____
_____

Places lived (most current to first home) _____
_____

Religious affiliations _____

Honors & achievements _____

Other interesting facts and stories _____
_____

1942
The U.S. builds its first atomic reactor.

OTHER ANCESTOR'S HISTORY

Ancestor's
photo goes
here

Relationship _____

Full name _____

Date of birth _____

Place of birth _____

Size at birth _____

Hair color _____

Eye color _____

Mother's full name _____

Father's full name _____

Siblings (name & date of birth) _____
_____

Marriage (date, place and special notes) _____
_____

Children (name[s] and birthdate[s]) _____
_____

Schools, degrees, courses of study _____
_____

Occupation[s] and employment (including military service) _____
_____
_____

Places lived (most current to first home) _____
_____

Religious affiliations _____

Honors & achievements _____

Other interesting facts and stories _____
_____
_____

December 7, 1941
The Japanese attack Pearl Harbor, Hawaii. The
U.S. and Britain then declare war on Japan.

OTHER ANCESTOR'S HISTORY

Ancestor's photo goes here

Relationship _____

Full name _____

Date of birth _____

Place of birth _____

Size at birth _____

Hair color _____

Eye color _____

Mother's full name _____

Father's full name _____

Siblings (name & date of birth) _____

_____

Marriage (date, place and special notes) _____

Children (name[s] and birthdate[s]) _____

Schools, degrees, courses of study _____

Occupation[s] and employment (including military service) _____

_____

Places lived (most current to first home) _____

_____

Religious affiliations _____

Honors & achievements _____

Other interesting facts and stories _____

_____

1940
The 40s were the Big Band era, and teenagers emerged as a separately identified demographic group dubbed bobby-soxers by the press.

OTHER ANCESTOR'S HISTORY

Ancestor's
photo goes
here

Relationship _____

Full name _____

Date of birth _____

Place of birth _____

Size at birth _____

Hair color _____

Eye color _____

Mother's full name _____

Father's full name _____

Siblings (name & date of birth) _____

_____

Marriage (date, place and special notes) _____

Children (name[s] and birthdate[s]) _____

Schools, degrees, courses of study _____

Occupation[s] and employment (including military service) _____

_____

Places lived (most current to first home) _____

_____

Religious affiliations _____

Honors & achievements _____

Other interesting facts and stories _____

_____

1939
The mega-hit film "Gone With the Wind" is released.

OTHER ANCESTOR'S HISTORY

Ancestor's
photo goes
here

Relationship _____

Full name _____

Date of birth _____

Place of birth _____

Size at birth _____

Hair color _____

Eye color _____

Mother's full name _____

Father's full name _____

Siblings (name & date of birth) _____

_____

Marriage (date, place and special notes) _____

Children (name[s] and birthdate[s]) _____

Schools, degrees, courses of study _____

Occupation[s] and employment (including military service) _____

_____

Places lived (most current to first home) _____

_____

Religious affiliations _____

Honors & achievements _____

Other interesting facts and stories _____

_____

April 30, 1939
The National Broadcasting Company (NBC) begins the
first regular television service in the U.S.

OTHER ANCESTOR'S HISTORY

Ancestor's
photo goes
here

Relationship _____

Full name _____

Date of birth _____

Place of birth _____

Size at birth _____

Hair color _____

Eye color _____

Mother's full name _____

Father's full name _____

Siblings (name & date of birth) _____

_____

Marriage (date, place and special notes) _____

Children (name[s] and birthdate[s]) _____

Schools, degrees, courses of study _____

Occupation[s] and employment (including military service) _____

_____

Places lived (most current to first home) _____

_____

Religious affiliations _____

Honors & achievements _____

Other interesting facts and stories _____

_____

October 31, 1938
Orson Welles narrates "War of the Worlds" on a radio broadcast, and terror of invaders from space sweeps the country as many listeners believe it is real.

OTHER ANCESTOR'S HISTORY

Ancestor's
photo goes
here

Relationship _____

Full name _____

Date of birth _____

Place of birth _____

Size at birth _____

Hair color _____

Eye color _____

Mother's full name _____

Father's full name _____

Siblings (name & date of birth) _____

_____

Marriage (date, place and special notes) _____

_____

Children (name[s] and birthdate[s]) _____

_____

Schools, degrees, courses of study _____

_____

Occupation[s] and employment (including military service) _____

_____

_____

Places lived (most current to first home) _____

_____

_____

Religious affiliations _____

_____

Honors & achievements _____

_____

Other interesting facts and stories _____

_____

_____

_____

September 1, 1939
German armies invade Poland. Britain and France declare
war on Germany on September 3.

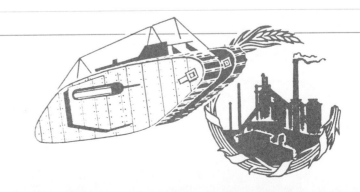

OTHER ANCESTOR'S HISTORY

Ancestor's
photo goes
here

Relationship _____

Full name _____

Date of birth _____

Place of birth _____

Size at birth _____

Hair color _____

Eye color _____

Mother's full name _____

Father's full name _____

Siblings (name & date of birth) _____

_____

Marriage (date, place and special notes) _____

_____

Children (name[s] and birthdate[s]) _____

_____

Schools, degrees, courses of study _____

_____

Occupation[s] and employment (including military service) _____

_____

_____

Places lived (most current to first home) _____

_____

_____

Religious affiliations _____

_____

Honors & achievements _____

_____

Other interesting facts and stories _____

1934
The "Zephyr" hits the nation's railways as America's first streamlined train.

OTHER ANCESTOR'S HISTORY

Ancestor's
photo goes
here

Relationship _____

Full name _____

Date of birth _____

Place of birth _____

Size at birth _____

Hair color _____

Eye color _____

Mother's full name _____

Father's full name _____

Siblings (name & date of birth) _____

_____

Marriage (date, place and special notes) _____

Children (name[s] and birthdate[s]) _____

Schools, degrees, courses of study _____

Occupation[s] and employment (including military service) _____

_____

Places lived (most current to first home) _____

_____

Religious affiliations _____

Honors & achievements _____

Other interesting facts and stories _____

August 14, 1935
The Social Security Act takes effect to provide pensions for
65-and-older workers.

75

DEATHS

Name _____ Date _____

Place of burial _____ Cause of death _____

Name _____ Date _____

Place of burial _____ Cause of death _____

Name _____ Date _____

Place of burial _____ Cause of death _____

Name _____ Date _____

Place of burial _____ Cause of death _____

Name _____ Date _____

Place of burial _____ Cause of death _____

Name _____ Date _____

Place of burial _____ Cause of death _____

Name _____ Date _____

Place of burial _____ Cause of death _____

Name _____ Date _____

Place of burial _____ Cause of death _____

Name _____ Date _____

Place of burial _____ Cause of death _____

1934
Shirley Temple sings and dances her way to stardom. She becomes the country's top movie draw from 1935-38.

Name _____ Date _____

Place of burial _____ Cause of death _____

Name _____ Date _____

Place of burial _____ Cause of death _____

Name _____ Date _____

Place of burial _____ Cause of death _____

Name _____ Date _____

Place of burial _____ Cause of death _____

Name _____ Date _____

Place of burial _____ Cause of death _____

Name _____ Date _____

Place of burial _____ Cause of death _____

Name _____ Date _____

Place of burial _____ Cause of death _____

Name _____ Date _____

Place of burial _____ Cause of death _____

Name _____ Date _____

Place of burial _____ Cause of death _____

December 5, 1933
Prohibition is repealed.

RELIGIOUS EVENTS

Name _____ Date _____ Place _____

Event / Ceremony _____

Name _____ Date _____ Place _____

Event / Ceremony _____

Name _____ Date _____ Place _____

Event / Ceremony _____

Name _____ Date _____ Place _____

Event / Ceremony _____

Name _____ Date _____ Place _____

Event / Ceremony _____

Name _____ Date _____ Place _____

Event / Ceremony _____

Name _____ Date _____ Place _____

Event / Ceremony _____

Name _____ Date _____ Place _____

Event / Ceremony _____

Name _____ Date _____ Place _____

Event / Ceremony _____

Name _____ Date _____ Place _____

Event / Ceremony _____

Name _____ Date _____ Place _____

Event / Ceremony _____

January 30, 1933
Adolf Hitler becomes Chancellor of Germany.

Name_____ Date_____ Place_____

Event / Ceremony_____

Name_____ Date_____ Place_____

Event / Ceremony_____

Name_____ Date_____ Place_____

Event / Ceremony_____

Name_____ Date_____ Place_____

Event / Ceremony_____

Name_____ Date_____ Place_____

Event / Ceremony_____

Name_____ Date_____ Place_____

Event / Ceremony_____

Name_____ Date_____ Place_____

Event / Ceremony_____

Name_____ Date_____ Place_____

Event / Ceremony_____

Name_____ Date_____ Place_____

Event / Ceremony_____

Name_____ Date_____ Place_____

Event / Ceremony_____

Name_____ Date_____ Place_____

Event / Ceremony_____

March 4, 1933

Franklin D. Roosevelt takes office as the 32nd President. This same day the U.S. banking system collapsed and banks across the country closed their doors. Roosevelt soon instituted his "New Deal" programs.

FAMILY EVENTS

Note here occasions to remember, great or small, that do not fall under other headings.

What _____ When _____
Who _____

What _____ When _____
Who _____

What _____ When _____
Who _____

What _____ When _____
Who _____

What _____ When _____
Who _____

What _____ When _____
Who _____

What _____ When _____
Who _____

What _____ When _____
Who _____

What _____ When _____
Who _____

What _____ When _____
Who _____

The 1930s
The Great Depression — breadlines, apples sold on stre
corners, estimates of 25% of the work force unemploy

What _____ When _____
Who _____

What _____ When _____
Who _____

What _____ When _____
Who _____

What _____ When _____
Who _____

What _____ When _____
Who _____

What _____ When _____
Who _____

What _____ When _____
Who _____

What _____ When _____
Who _____

What _____ When _____
Who _____

What _____ When _____
Who _____

What _____ When _____
Who _____

1930
Supermarkets and frozen foods begin to appear.

FAMILY EVENTS

What_____ When_____
Who_____

What_____ When_____
Who_____

What_____ When_____
Who_____

What_____ When_____
Who_____

What_____ When_____
Who_____

What_____ When_____
Who_____

What_____ When_____
Who_____

What_____ When_____
Who_____

What_____ When_____
Who_____

What_____ When_____
Who_____

What_____ When_____
Who_____

1928 Penicillin, the first antibiotic, is discovered by Alexander Fleming.

What _____ When _____
Who _____

What _____ When _____
Who _____

What _____ When _____
Who _____

What _____ When _____
Who _____

What _____ When _____
Who _____

What _____ When _____
Who _____

What _____ When _____
Who _____

What _____ When _____
Who _____

What _____ When _____
Who _____

What _____ When _____
Who _____

May 21, 1927
Charles Lindbergh arrives in France, completing the first solo nonstop flight across the Atlantic.

83

FAMILY VACATIONS

Where_____ When_____
Who went_____
Notes_____

Where_____ When_____
Who went_____
Notes_____

Where_____ When_____
Who went_____
Notes_____

Where_____ When_____
Who went_____
Notes_____

Where_____ When_____
Who went_____
Notes_____

Where_____ When_____
Who went_____
Notes_____

Where_____ When_____
Who went_____
Notes_____

Where_____ When_____
Who went_____
Notes_____

1927 New York Yankees' star Babe Ruth has his best-ever season with a total of 60 home runs.

Where _____ When _____
Who went _____
Notes _____

Where _____ When _____
Who went _____
Notes _____

Where _____ When _____
Who went _____
Notes _____

Where _____ When _____
Who went _____
Notes _____

Where _____ When _____
Who went _____
Notes _____

Where _____ When _____
Who went _____
Notes _____

Where _____ When _____
Who went _____
Notes _____

Where _____ When _____
Who went _____
Notes _____

March 16, 1926
The first liquid-fuel rocket is successfully launched, beginning the space age.

FAMILY GATHERINGS

Occasion _____ Date _____

Who attended _____

_____

_____

Notes _____

Occasion _____ Date _____

Who attended _____

_____

_____

Notes _____

Occasion _____ Date _____

Who attended _____

_____

_____

Notes _____

Occasion _____ Date _____

Who attended _____

_____

_____

Notes _____

Occasion _____ Date _____

Who attended _____

_____

_____

Notes _____

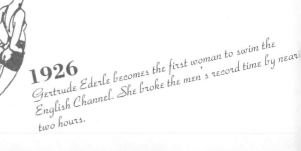

1926 Gertrude Ederle becomes the first woman to swim the English Channel. She broke the men's record time by near two hours.

Occasion _____ Date _____

Who attended _____

_____

_____

Notes _____

Occasion _____ Date _____

Who attended _____

_____

_____

Notes _____

Occasion _____ Date _____

Who attended _____

_____

_____

Notes _____

Occasion _____ Date _____

Who attended _____

_____

_____

Notes _____

Occasion _____ Date _____

Who attended _____

_____

Notes _____

1925 Louis "Satchmo" Armstrong transforms jazz in the age of jazz.

FAMILY GATHERINGS 🏠

Occasion _____ Date _____

Who attended _____

_____

Notes _____

Occasion _____ Date _____

Who attended _____

_____

Notes _____

Occasion _____ Date _____

Who attended _____

_____

Notes _____

Occasion _____ Date _____

Who attended _____

_____

Notes _____

Occasion _____ Date _____

Who attended _____

_____

Notes _____

1925 The famous Scopes trial found biology teacher John T. Scopes guilty of teaching Darwin's theory of evolution.

Occasion _____ Date _____

Who attended _____

_____

_____

Notes _____

Occasion _____ Date _____

Who attended _____

_____

_____

Notes _____

Occasion _____ Date _____

Who attended _____

_____

_____

Notes _____

Occasion _____ Date _____

Who attended _____

_____

_____

Notes _____

Occasion _____ Date _____

Who attended _____

_____

_____

Notes _____

December 30, 1922
The Union of Soviet Socialist Republics is established.

FAMILY TRADITIONS

Record traditions your family observes at holidays, birthdays, or other special occasions. When known, note with whom, where and when a tradition began.

A tradition of _____ Observed _____

_____

_____

A tradition of _____ Observed _____

_____

_____

A tradition of _____ Observed _____

_____

_____

A tradition of _____ Observed _____

_____

_____

A tradition of _____ Observed _____

_____

_____

A tradition of _____ Observed _____

_____

_____

A tradition of _____ Observed _____

_____

_____

1922
Car radios are invented.

A tradition of _____ Observed _____
_____
_____

A tradition of _____ Observed _____
_____
_____

A tradition of _____ Observed _____
_____
_____

A tradition of _____ Observed _____
_____
_____

A tradition of _____ Observed _____
_____
_____

A tradition of _____ Observed _____
_____
_____

A tradition of _____ Observed _____
_____
_____

January 16, 1920
Prohibition begins and so does the rise of illegal alcohol served in "speakeasies."

HEIRLOOMS & FAMILY PAPERS

List here important family heirlooms and documents, who owns them, where they are kept and to whom they will go.

Item _____   Owner _____
Location _____   Goes to _____

Item _____   Owner _____
Location _____   Goes to _____

Item _____   Owner _____
Location _____   Goes to _____

Item _____   Owner _____
Location _____   Goes to _____

Item _____   Owner _____
Location _____   Goes to _____

Item _____   Owner _____
Location _____   Goes to _____

Item _____   Owner _____
Location _____   Goes to _____

Item _____   Owner _____
Location _____   Goes to _____

Item _____   Owner _____
Location _____   Goes to _____

Item _____   Owner _____
Location _____   Goes to _____

January 10, 1920
The League of Nations comes into being.

Item	Owner
Location	Goes to
Item	Owner
Location	Goes to
Item	Owner
Location	Goes to
Item	Owner
Location	Goes to
Item	Owner
Location	Goes to
Item	Owner
Location	Goes to
Item	Owner
Location	Goes to
Item	Owner
Location	Goes to
Item	Owner
Location	Goes to
Item	Owner
Location	Goes to
Item	Owner
Location	Goes to

The 1920s

Flappers, bootleg gin, women's bobbed hair, mobsters, and the age of jazz.

IMPORTANT FAMILY DATES

JANUARY

1

2

3

4

5

6

7

8

9

10

11

12

13

14

15

16

17

18

19

20

21

22

23

24

25

26

27

28

29

30

31

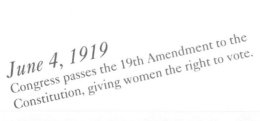

June 4, 1919
Congress passes the 19th Amendment to the
Constitution, giving women the right to vote.

FEBRUARY

1	16
2	17
3	18
4	19
5	20
6	21
7	22
8	23
9	24
10	25
11	26
12	27
13	28
14	29
15	

November 11, 1918
German delegates sign an armistice ending
World War I.

M A R C H

1 _____
2 _____
3 _____
4 _____
5 _____
6 _____
7 _____
8 _____
9 _____
10 _____
11 _____
12 _____
13 _____
14 _____
15 _____

16 _____
17 _____
18 _____
19 _____
20 _____
21 _____
22 _____
23 _____
24 _____
25 _____
26 _____
27 _____
28 _____
29 _____
30 _____
31 _____

April 2, 1917
President Woodrow Wilson calls for a declaration of war on Germany.

APRIL

1 _____

2 _____

3 _____

4 _____

5 _____

6 _____

7 _____

8 _____

9 _____

10 _____

11 _____

12 _____

13 _____

14 _____

15 _____

16 _____

17 _____

18 _____

19 _____

20 _____

21 _____

22 _____

23 _____

24 _____

25 _____

26 _____

27 _____

28 _____

29 _____

30 _____

1917
Czar Nicholas II is overthrown
in Russia.

M A Y

1 _____

2 _____

3 _____

4 _____

5 _____

6 _____

7 _____

8 _____

9 _____

10 _____

11 _____

12 _____

13 _____

14 _____

15 _____

16 _____

17 _____

18 _____

19 _____

20 _____

21 _____

22 _____

23 _____

24 _____

25 _____

26 _____

27 _____

28 _____

29 _____

30 _____

31 _____

1916
Mary Pickford is the world's best-loved actress and is dubbed "America's Sweetheart."

JUNE

1 _____

2 _____

3 _____

4 _____

5 _____

6 _____

7 _____

8 _____

9 _____

10 _____

11 _____

12 _____

13 _____

14 _____

15 _____

16 _____

17 _____

18 _____

19 _____

20 _____

21 _____

22 _____

23 _____

24 _____

25 _____

26 _____

27 _____

28 _____

29 _____

30 _____

1916
Congress creates the National Park Service to impose hunting limits on the newly mobile population.

JULY

1 _____

2 _____

3 _____

4 _____

5 _____

6 _____

7 _____

8 _____

9 _____

10 _____

11 _____

12 _____

13 _____

14 _____

15 _____

16 _____

17 _____

18 _____

19 _____

20 _____

21 _____

22 _____

23 _____

24 _____

25 _____

26 _____

27 _____

28 _____

29 _____

30 _____

31 _____

1916
Ford's Model T becomes priced right for the general public: mass production drops the price to $360 each.

AUGUST

1
2
3
4
5
6
7
8
9
10
11
12
13
14
15

16
17
18
19
20
21
22
23
24
25
26
27
28
29
30
31

August 15, 1914
The Panama Canal is officially opened.

SEPTEMBER

1 _____
_____
2 _____
_____
3 _____
_____
4 _____
_____
5 _____
_____
6 _____
_____
7 _____
_____
8 _____
_____
9 _____
_____
10 _____
_____
11 _____
_____
12 _____
_____
13 _____
_____
14 _____
_____
15 _____
_____

16 _____
_____
17 _____
_____
18 _____
_____
19 _____
_____
20 _____
_____
21 _____
_____
22 _____
_____
23 _____
_____
24 _____
_____
25 _____
_____
26 _____
_____
27 _____
_____
28 _____
_____
29 _____
_____
30 _____
_____

July 28, 1914
War breaks out in Europe between Austria-Hungary and Serbia. It is the beginning of what will become World War I.

OCTOBER

1 _____

2 _____

3 _____

4 _____

5 _____

6 _____

7 _____

8 _____

9 _____

10 _____

11 _____

12 _____

13 _____

14 _____

15 _____

16 _____

17 _____

18 _____

19 _____

20 _____

21 _____

22 _____

23 _____

24 _____

25 _____

26 _____

27 _____

28 _____

29 _____

30 _____

31 _____

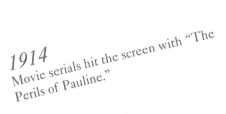

1914
Movie serials hit the screen with "The
Perils of Pauline."

NOVEMBER

1 _____

2 _____

3 _____

4 _____

5 _____

6 _____

7 _____

8 _____

9 _____

10 _____

11 _____

12 _____

13 _____

14 _____

15 _____

16 _____

17 _____

18 _____

19 _____

20 _____

21 _____

22 _____

23 _____

24 _____

25 _____

26 _____

27 _____

28 _____

29 _____

30 _____

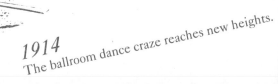

1914
The ballroom dance craze reaches new heights.

DECEMBER

1 _____ 16 _____

2 _____ 17 _____

3 _____ 18 _____

4 _____ 19 _____

5 _____ 20 _____

6 _____ 21 _____

7 _____ 22 _____

8 _____ 23 _____

9 _____ 24 _____

10 _____ 25 _____

11 _____ 26 _____

12 _____ 27 _____

13 _____ 28 _____

14 _____ 29 _____

15 _____ 30 _____

31 _____

1913
Cecil B. deMille arrives in Hollywood to make his
first movie, "Squaw Man."

SIGNATURES

Signatures of family members can be recorded here for historical preservation.
Space has been provided for you to print the name of the person giving the autograph
and the date it is written.

Printed name_____ Date_____

Signature_____

Printed name_____ Date_____

Signature_____

Printed name_____ Date_____

Signature_____

Printed name_____ Date_____

Signature_____

Printed name_____ Date_____

Signature_____

Printed name_____ Date_____

Signature_____

Printed name_____ Date_____

Signature_____

Printed name_____ Date_____

Signature_____

Printed name_____ Date_____

Signature_____

February 25, 1913
Federal income tax becomes law in the U.S. under
the 16th Amendment.

Printed name _____ Date _____

Signature _____

Printed name _____ Date _____

Signature _____

Printed name _____ Date _____

Signature _____

Printed name _____ Date _____

Signature _____

Printed name _____ Date _____

Signature _____

Printed name _____ Date _____

Signature _____

Printed name _____ Date _____

Signature _____

Printed name _____ Date _____

Signature _____

Printed name _____ Date _____

Signature _____

Printed name _____ Date _____

Signature _____

1913
"The Saturday Evening Post" was the country's
top magazine with a circulation of 2 million.

SIGNATURES

Printed name _____ Date _____
Signature _____

Printed name _____ Date _____
Signature _____

Printed name _____ Date _____
Signature _____

Printed name _____ Date _____
Signature _____

Printed name _____ Date _____
Signature _____

Printed name _____ Date _____
Signature _____

Printed name _____ Date _____
Signature _____

Printed name _____ Date _____
Signature _____

Printed name _____ Date _____
Signature _____

Printed name _____ Date _____
Signature _____

November 5, 1912
Woodrow Wilson defeats incumbent President William H. Taft.

Printed name _____ Date _____

Signature _____

Printed name _____ Date _____

Signature _____

Printed name _____ Date _____

Signature _____

Printed name _____ Date _____

Signature _____

Printed name _____ Date _____

Signature _____

Printed name _____ Date _____

Signature _____

Printed name _____ Date _____

Signature _____

Printed name _____ Date _____

Signature _____

Printed name _____ Date _____

Signature _____

Printed name _____ Date _____

Signature _____

In the decade of the 1910s
Personal cameras and picture-taking take hold.
Chautauguas (inspirational tent shows) were the
most popular summertime cultural events across
the country.

ORAL HISTORY NOTES

Person interviewed _____ Date _____

Age at time of interview _____ Place of interview _____

Notes _____

_____

_____

_____

_____

_____

_____

_____

_____

Person interviewed _____ Date _____

Age at time of interview _____ Place of interview _____

Notes _____

_____

_____

_____

_____

_____

_____

_____

1908
Henry Ford produces the Model T, the "Tin Lizzie." It costs
$850. Mass-production processes are born.

Person interviewed _____ Date _____

Age at time of interview _____ Place of interview _____

Notes _____
_____
_____
_____
_____
_____
_____
_____
_____
_____
_____

Person interviewed _____ Date _____

Age at time of interview _____ Place of interview _____

Notes _____
_____
_____
_____
_____
_____
_____
_____
_____
_____
_____
_____

December 24, 1906
The first radio broadcast of the human voice and music was
made by inventor Reginald Fessenden.

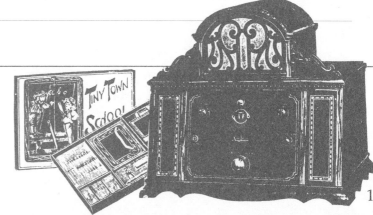

ORAL HISTORY NOTES

Person interviewed _____ Date _____

Age at time of interview _____ Place of interview _____

Notes _____
_____
_____
_____
_____
_____
_____
_____
_____
_____
_____
_____

Person interviewed _____ Date _____

Age at time of interview _____ Place of interview _____

Notes _____
_____
_____
_____
_____
_____
_____
_____
_____
_____
_____

1905
The first nickelodeon (moving picture theater) was opened. By
1910, local theaters were drawing 10 million people a week.

Person interviewed _____ Date _____

Age at time of interview _____ Place of interview _____

Notes _____

_____

_____

_____

_____

_____

_____

_____

_____

_____

Person interviewed _____ Date _____

Age at time of interview _____ Place of interview _____

Notes _____

_____

_____

_____

_____

_____

_____

_____

_____

1905
Albert Einstein publishes his special theory of relativity,
forever altering our concepts of time and space.

113

OTHER NOTES

December 17, 1903
The "Flyer," launched by Wilbur and Orville Wright, becomes the first successful self-propelled aircraft.

1903
The first successful U.S. feature film, "The Great Train Robbery," involves audiences in a new way by showing a bandit shooting directly into the audience.

OTHER NOTES

1902
Marie Curie, who coined the term "radioactivity," is the first to isolate pure radium.

1902
"In the Good Old Summertime" becomes one of the most popular songs of the era, selling a million copies in a single year.

OTHER NOTES

1901
Hemlines rise to just above the ankle and bustles fall from fashion.

1900
Spanish-American War hero Theodore Roosevelt becomes
Vice President on the ticket of President William McKinley.
He takes over as President when McKinley is assassinated
less than one year later.

PHOTOGRAPHS & MEMORABILIA

RESOURCES FOR FAMILY HISTORY

Many excellent books have been written detailing how to thoroughly research your family tree. Look under "Genealogy" in the card catalog of your local library. You are sure to find at least a few of these detailed guides available to you. Here, however, is a general list of ways to begin your search for your own family history:

1. Talk to every living relative that you know. Ask them if they can fill in any blanks in your family ancestral charts.

2. Find out if anyone in the family has a Family Bible that has been passed down through generations. Many of the names and dates that you will need might be found in that one source.

3. Find and read old letters, newspaper clippings and the notes on photographs which belong or belonged to older relatives. Old trunks in attics and basements are notorious stashes for these bits of information.

4. With a few names as a starting point, go to the courthouse of the county in which your ancestors lived. Birth, marriage and death records may be intact there.

5. Talk with the librarian in your local library or the nearest university library. Ask about special genealogical collections or data. Find the address for your state's bureau of vital statistics. State Bureaus of Vital Statistics are often a storehouse of information that you need.

6. Check your phone directory or local chamber of commerce to find community genealogical societies or historical societies. These societies should be able to help you with additional information or sources.

7. Check with the office of a cemetery where you believe ancestors are buried. Their records may be surprisingly helpful.

8. When the church affiliation of past generations is known, research church records.

9. Federal Census Records from 1790-1910 are open for public inspection. Your local or regional library may have area census records on microfilm.

10. Find out which National Archives regional branch is nearest you. The National Archives in Washington D.C., is this country's central depository of records.

11. The library of the Church of Jesus Christ of Latter-Day Saints in Salt Lake City holds one of the largest collections of genealogical records in the world. They have genealogical documents from more than 40 countries. Several branches are maintained around the country, so you may want to contact them to find the branch nearest you.